KABALEVSKY
24 PIECES FOR CHILDREN
Opus 39

T0039742

Edited by Margaret Otwell

Also available:
00296691 Kabalevsky: 24 Pieces for Children, Opus 39,
with companion recordings by Margaret Otwell

On the cover:
Old Town II
by Wassily Kandinsky
(1866-1944)

ISBN: 978-1-4950-0734-7

G. SCHIRMER, Inc.

DISTRIBUTED BY

HAL•LEONARD®
CORPORATION

7777 W. BLUEMOUND RD. P.O. BOX 13819 MILWAUKEE, WI 53213

www.musicsalesclassical.com
www.halleonard.com

CONTENTS

HISTORICAL NOTES

DMITRI KABALEVSKY (1904-1987)

Dmitri Kabalevsky was born in St. Petersburg, Russia on December 30, 1904. He received a liberal education from his father. As a boy Dmitri excelled in the arts. He wrote poetry and painted, in addition to being an aspiring pianist. In 1918, at the age of 14, his family moved to Moscow where Kabalevsky enrolled in the Scriabin Music School. However, not unlike other parents of artists at the time, Kabalevsky's father wished him to pursue a career outside of the arts. In 1922, Kabalevsky took the entrance exam to the Engels Socio-Economic Science Institute, where he would likely pursue a career in mathematics or economics, like his father. Young Dmitri never enrolled in the school, however, and was determined to pursue a career in music.

In 1925, Kabalevsky went to the Moscow Conservatory to continue studies in piano and composition. His composition teacher was the well known composer Nikolai Miaskovsky, who had a significant impact on Kabalevsky's development. While there, he composed the first works to be recognized internationally: the Piano Concerto No. 1 (1928), and the Sonatina in C major (1930) for piano. He eventually became a full professor at the Moscow Conservatory in 1939.

Kabalevsky is best known outside of Russia for his numerous student works for piano. He first taught piano at the Scriabin Music School, where he composed works for his students, establishing a lifelong interest in providing young musicians with quality literature. In addition to the *24 Pieces for Children*, Opus 39, his other works for students include *30 Pieces for Children*, Opus 27, *Easy Variations*, Opus 40, *Five Easy Variations on Folk Themes*, Opus 51, and *35 Easy Pieces*, Opus 89, among others. These compositions are still widely taught today not only for their pedagogical value, but also for their musical freshness and appeal.

Kabalevsky had a successful career as a composer in the USSR due to a conservative aesthetic temperament, avoiding the difficulties encountered by his contemporaries Sergei Prokofiev and Dmitri Shostakovich, while still producing a large body of original music. Even so, following the 1948 party decree on music in the Soviet Union, Kabalevsky's works became significantly more lyrical in quality. It was during this period that he composed three concertos for young performers, including works for violin (1948), violoncello (1948-9) and the Concerto No. 3 for Piano (1952). His later pieces included many large works for chorus and orchestra, for which he remains most known in his native country. His orchestral works, concertos, and particularly his piano music brought him notoriety in the United States. Kabalevsky died in Moscow on February 18, 1987.

PERFORMANCE NOTES

The charming inventiveness of Kabalevsky's *24 Pieces for Children*, Opus 39, has made this collection a favorite source of piano teaching repertoire since their first publication in Russia in the 1930s. The long popularity of these delightful miniatures attests to Kabalevsky's talent, not only as a gifted composer, but also as a musician and pianist keenly interested in educating young musicians. In fact, he began composing in his teens, and many of his easier piano solos were written for his own students. The wide range of expressiveness and exploration of varied dynamics, tempos, and articulations in these solos provide valuable opportunities for the late-elementary and early-intermediate student to hone his musical abilities. Several pieces in this collection are true "character pieces," descriptive and finely crafted. They are a contemporary version of the type of piano solo made so famous by many Romantic-era composers. Although these short solos are for the most part artfully simple, it is readily apparent that they were not lightly tossed off, but were created with loving attention to detail, to their aesthetic beauty, and lastly, to their worthiness as teaching repertoire.

Kabalevsky was a master composer/pianist. The pieces in Opus 39 focus ingeniously on essential technical and interpretive skills within the context of imaginative, original works that are progressive in nature. The first 12 pieces are short, late-elementary works that effectively teach essential piano skills—basic articulation, dynamics, and phrasing—in accessible keys. The last 12 are slightly longer, and the technical, rhythmic, and musical challenges increase. These latter pieces fall in the early-intermediate range. The key signatures never venture beyond two flats (B-flat Major/G minor) and four sharps (E Major). All keys that intermediate pianists should be comfortable playing are reinforced throughout: C, Am, G, Em, D, Bm, A, E, F, Dm, and B-flat.

Kabalevsky's colorful music and the descriptive titles they bear invite a creative approach to 0interpretation within a clearly defined pedagogical framework, one that focuses on the skills every novice pianist must master. Students will find that these miniatures "feel good under the hand," and so they will gain physical confidence at the keyboard, thus earning a positive sense of accomplishment after learning any of them. Moreover, grouped together, these solos make excellent recital material, provided care is taken to vary the tempos, keys, and moods.

Piano students are apt to first encounter pieces from Opus 39 in teaching anthologies. The solos most often selected for elementary anthologies include many of the shorter pieces found at the beginning of the collection, among them No. 6, *A Little Joke*, No. 7, *Funny Event*, No. 8, *Song*, No. 9, *A Little Dance*, and No. 12, *Scherzo*. Anthologies for the intermediate pianist often contain selections from the later pieces in Opus 39, the more popular being No. 13, *Waltz*, No. 17, *Folk Dance*, No. 18, *Galop*, No. 20, *Clowns*, and No. 22, *A Short Story*. This brief encounter with Kabalevsky's *24 Pieces for Children* is the norm, regrettably so, for most piano students will move on in their studies without ever discovering the abundant inventiveness of the entire collection. Young performers who reach an intermediate stage of piano study are generally in a hurry to move on to more demanding repertoire, but there is much to be gained, technically and artistically, from studying many of the solos in this collection at a leisurely pace. This is music that can be polished to recital readiness in a few months, savored for its elegant finesse, and thoroughly enjoyed by students and their parents, adult students, and teachers. It is the sort of music that can inspire a student to dig deeply and to find new skills and musical insight in order to perform it well.

The Individual Works

Melody

This simple, straightforward piece should be played with careful attention to dynamic balance between the hands. Close regard to the phrasing in the melody, lifting the hand gently at the end of each marked slur, will make this short work more beautiful and tender. The blocked intervals in the left hand should be played with a smooth *legato*, even if the performer must stretch slightly to accomplish this. Slightly is the key word in that sentence—adding very light damper pedal is warranted as an alternative for children whose hands are truly too small to stretch the intervals. The decision to add pedal is an individual teacher's choice, but I would rather advocate adding it when needed, than to suggest that students struggle with *legato* chord playing before their hands are developed enough to do so comfortably. Since these pieces are often played by very young students, this issue needs to be considered, not only for this particular solo, but for others in the book as well.

Polka

This piece frolics along happily in great contrast to the first solo, with its jolly left-hand melody set against the right-hand *staccato* accompaniment. Care must be taken to assure that the performer plays the opposing articulations in each hand accurately and distinctly. Because of their highly contrasted tempos and characters, *Melody* and *Polka* make a great pairing for a student's first recital.

Rambling

In this short piece the performer must distinguish between *staccato*, *portato*, and *tenuto*—three very different types of non-legato touches. A novice pianist will find these touches easier to master if he/she practices some preliminary five-finger or scale exercises that emphasize these touches, so that a good physical feel for each type of touch becomes instinctive. The exercise can be simple: For example, play a D minor five-finger pattern hands together, first *staccato*, next *portato*, and then *tenuto*. Then play different articulations in each hand until playing two kinds of articulation at the same time becomes easy. Isolating the first beat only (RH *staccato*/LH *portato*) until one succeeds in making the touches sufficiently different will help to remind the fingers what to do when practice begins on the piece itself. Imagery, such as thinking of a portato touch as "pressing firmly into soft clay and then letting go,"

may help less experienced performers sense the difference between this *semi-staccato* touch and a true *staccato*.

Cradle Song

The two-note slur is introduced here in eighth notes. It is used to sharpen a fairly challenging technical skill: extending the fingers outward from a five-finger position to the octave and learning to sense the interval distances of the octave, 7th, 6th, and 5th without stretching to reach them. The visual image of the two-note slur counteracts a student's natural tendency to stretch while holding onto the lower note. It is very important to remind students to lift and place, rather than stretch when playing wide distances before the hand has grown large enough to reach them comfortably.

The tempo chosen for the solo is important, too. The overall tempo must be slow enough for the slurs never to feel rushed. The gentle leaps between the slurs will become ragged if the tempo is too fast. The hand should lift almost imperceptibly at the end of each slur, without a noticeable shortening of the note itself or an accent, floating seamlessly to the first note of the next slur. Imagining a gently swaying cradle may help students to master the subtle lateral wrist-motion needed in this solo.

Playing

This delightful solo is a great example of what I like to call a "touch piece." The continuous quarter-note *staccato* pattern alternates between the hand and imbues the whole piece with a happy, carefree personality. The focus is entirely on the articulation, which is constantly *staccato*, excepting the very last note. One can almost imagine two squirrels chasing each other up and down a tree at top speed. That kind of imagery may help a young student understand how the hands must follow each other without pause. The technical challenge lies in creating an unwavering, steady pulse from the very first note to the very last, with no hesitation when the right or left hand assumes leadership as the music falls and rises in the first few measures, answers back and forth in opposing motion in the middle phrase, and finally tumbles downward, only to rise once more at the very end. The translated title, *Playing*, doesn't truly convey the effervescent quality of this solo. Students must feel free to inject lots of energy and pure joy into their performance. They can do that only if they know exactly where the line is going at all times. Steady, slow practice, only gradually working up to a sparkling tempo, will guarantee success.

A Little Joke

A perennial favorite, with good reason, this capricious piece concentrates effectively on parallel motion between the hands. The melody is the same in both hands, and is marked by alternating two-note slurs and *staccato* notes, with *portato* notes at the cadence points. Care must be taken to differentiate these three touches throughout the piece. Although the only dynamic given is *mf* in the first measure, it makes sense to shape the dynamics in eight-bar phrases. The phrase at m. 9 could be played several ways. Two suggestions are to begin *f* and *decrescendo* to the end, or begin *mp* and *crescendo* to the very end. I prefer the latter.

Funny Event

The pianist plays "copy cat" in this solo—both hands alternate back and forth as the right hand imitates the exact notes, touches, and rhythms the left hand has just played. Students can be made aware of this detail by playing the right- and left-hand matching motives simultaneously, preferably *legato* and slowly.

This preliminary step also sharpens students' reading skills, asking them to take in two measures at once as they read through the solo. It is also a shortcut to learning the entire piece for students. If they understand the structure of this simple piece, they will not feel overwhelmed by the challenge of playing it correctly. Practicing the motives hands together and then alternately gives students a double technical workout, building finger independence in both hands, and honing rhythmic precision between the hands. Playing a long, sustained *crescendo* from the *p* at m. 9 to the *f* at m. 17 will keep the energy of the piece at a high level.

Song

The parallel melody in both hands is similar to *A Little Joke*, but this solo's tempo, key, and *legato* phrases suggest a serious mood, perhaps even sad. Kabalevsky uses the lower register of the piano very effectively here by placing the parallel melody in the left hand two octaves below the

right hand. Both hands therefore play in the richest register of the piano—from two octaves below Middle C through the Middle C octave. The resulting sound, rich in overtones, is round and full, even though the piece has no chords at all. The brief appearance of the major mode at m. 6 is startling, and must be an "event" arrived at purposefully, as should the wide leap of an octave in the last measure, the largest interval found in the piece. Because of their similar parallel writing, *Song* and *A Little Joke* make an excellent pairing on recital programs.

A Little Dance

This happy piece has the character of a lively folk dance. As such, it should be performed at a brisk tempo, but with a very steady pulse and great attention to the sharply contrasting dynamic levels throughout. The juxtaposition of the Gm7 and G7 harmonies in mm. 5–8 is highly colorful, and should be treated as an expressive opportunity in the piece. No *ritardando* at the end is needed; rather, the musical line should continue without the slightest sign of slowing down.

March

This solo explores a single rhythmic figure throughout in two-note slurs.

March, Op. 39, No. 10, mm. 1-3, r.h.

Keeping this figure precise while executing quick extensions and contractions the hand, motions needed to play the melody effortlessly, makes this piece a technical and rhythmic challenge for the novice player. Moreover, to give the right "swing" to the four-measure phrases, the tempo must be adequately brisk to propel the line downward in a tumbling motion. Notably, Kabalevsky places the slurs as the performer would instinctively play them—from short to long. Does this mean that the player should lift his hand after playing each dotted 16th? Perhaps! The slurs indicated throughout this book are very precise. Some are very short; others are noticeably longer. Kabalevsky could have written long slurs here, covering each four-measure phrase, but he chose shorter slurs. Personally, I like the feel of moving from the emphatic, outer fingers of the hand (5 and 4 in mm. 1-2) to the thumb when I played these passages, and so, in the recording I released my hand slightly between the slurs. The slight kick that this motion gives to the downbeat is satisfying and physically fun to play. A fast tempo allows the hand to flip along from slur to slur with a slightly detached touch between the slurs. This piece is very brief, and so possibly warrants a *f* dynamic throughout, as marked. However, the performer could experiment with a terraced dynamic plan as well: *f* from mm. 1–4; *p* from mm. 5-8; *f* from mm. 9-12; *mp* and *crescendo* to the end from m. 13 to the end.

Song of Autumn

Both hands share the same melody in *Song of Autumn*, just as they do in Opus 39, No. 8, *Song*. The similarities between these two beautiful solos are obvious at once: They are both set in a minor key and use parallel melodies; they are both wistful, expressive songs in a moderate tempo, and are played entirely *legato*. Perhaps Kabalevsky crafted this work as a corresponding sight-reading study to *Song*. Significantly, both solos explore new registers in either the bass or treble clef, and Kabalevsky cleverly encourages sure reading skills in each by pairing the new register with a known register that most elementary students would surely know. However, he reverses the challenge in each solo: In *Song*, low bass-clef notes are introduced, paired with a safe, mid-keyboard D-minor position in the right hand. In *Song of Autumn*, Kabalevsky positions the right hand on high treble-clef notes, while the left hand imitates the melody note-for-note in a familiar register in the bass clef. Given this correspondence, learning both pieces concurrently or sequentially would be very beneficial to most students.

The subtle, elegant difference between the two solos lies in their phrasing and meter: *Song* is in common time; the phrases always begin on the downbeat, and the slurs are placed over each full measure throughout. *Song of Autumn* is in 2/4 meter; the phrases begin on an upbeat, and the slurs vary in length from two beats to five. The implied stresses in each solo are therefore quite different. Although this may not sound momentous in writing, it is, as music. These pieces will sound quite dissimilar in performance due to these meter and phrasing differences. In *Song of Autumn* particularly, students must learn how to begin each motive with a gentle, unaccented touch, and lift their hands gently between each slur with only a slight breath.

Song of Autumn, Op. 39, No. 11, mm. 1-5, r.h.

Scherzo

Like *Playing* and *Funny Event*, *Scherzo* is an alternating-hands study. Its mono-rhythmic character also makes it a wonderful rhythm exercise. An additional challenge is that the student must play two different articulations between the hands: The left hand plays *legato* while the right hand plays *staccato*. These three challenges in one short piece sound deceptively simple on paper, but they can present the young performer with a good challenge and multiple opportunities to hone his skills. The tempo should match the spirit of the tempo indication, "*vivo, giocoso*," which means "lively and jocular."

Waltz

This is the first dance in 3/4 in the collection. The melody of this poignant waltz arches gracefully upwards with wide intervallic leaps, imparting a yearning quality that is quite expressive. Here, Kabalevsky increases the technical and interpretive challenges for the performer, but carefully so—the challenges lie only in the right hand, for the left hand plays a simple, double-note accompaniment on beats one and two. Students should be encouraged to play the beautiful melody with a smooth and lustrous *legato*.

A Fable

This excellent *staccato* study in A major lies easily under the hands in shifting five-finger positions. The *staccato* notes should be played precisely and lightly to reflect the happy, carefree mood of the solo, while the few contrasting *legato* motives should be played with equal attention. Note that two separate slurs comprise these *legato* motives. Lifting the hand lightly at the end of each slur will make this brief musical sketch even more expressive. The first two measures of the melody use a kind of "tucked in" thumb position: Finger 2 shifts back and forth between C# and E, while the thumb tucks under for the D. It is important to work out and practice slowly the fingering challenges and hand-position shifts posed by the A-Major key signature.

Jumping

This playful solo has a parallel melody whose notes are identical, but whose rhythms are not. This disparity may pose a coordinative challenge for novice players, for the rhythmic elements must be precise and each short motive must be clearly articulated throughout. Playing only beats one and two of each measure hands together in a slow tempo will help most young players get a good physical feel for the alternating hand's rhythmic "hiccup." It will help to point out that both hands leave the keyboard at the same time—on beat three. The brief minor excursion in mm. 9–16, marked *p*, provides an effective contrast to the ebullient beginning and its repeat at the end of the piece.

A Sad Story

Despite its brevity, this somber, pensive solo expresses sadness very beautifully and in an understated way. It is therefore an excellent piece for the novice pianist to learn patient and expressive playing in the *piano* to *pianissimo* dynamic range. At the beginning, the left hand carries the main melody while the right hand provides the embellishment. Nonetheless, the right-hand part is truly another melody that eventually joins in as a duet beginning at m. 8, and so it, too, plays an important role in creating the expressive mood of the piece. The left hand in mm. 1–8 and mm. 17–24 must be played with an unhurried, smooth *legato* touch, while the right-hand's two-note slurs add a kind of gentle, plaintive sigh. A slight lift on the last note of each slur in the right hand—one that also does not cheat the full value of the dotted half-note—will enhance the delicate quality of this haunting solo. In mm. 9–14 the parallel two-note slurs in both hands also should be played without cheating the full value of the half notes. A somewhat reluctant lift of the hand is called for here, as if the fingers were almost stuck to the keys.

Folk Dance

This rollicking canon in two voices moves along cheerfully at a brisk tempo with quick, light *staccato* eighths providing lots of forward movement and energy. The eighths throughout must be kept strictly in time—very metronomic—yet they must also have a carefree verve that gives the solo a sparkling, invigorated personality, ending in an exhilarating *crescendo* to the final, confident quarter notes at the very end. This solo is a superb recital piece. At the right tempo, it can give young players a marvelous first taste of "virtuoso" playing.

Galop

Like its predecessor, this outgoing solo may also be given to a young performer who is eager to sharpen his confidence and security at the keyboard. It is more difficult than *Folk Dance* because of the technically challenging broken chords in the left-hand and the wide leaps in the right-hand melody—both hands need to be played with supreme confidence. The rewards are great, however, for this piece can give intermediate players a great sense of accomplishment and it is truly exciting to perform. Care should be taken to play each two-note slur accurately in the broken-chord accompaniment, lifting the hand slightly on the last note of each slur and coming down on the two-note interval securely and with a full sound. The fifth finger should essentially "go along for the ride" while the main focus remains on the double notes. It also makes good sense to isolate the right-hand passage in mm. 5–7 to learn the interval distances of each motive precisely and securely. The leaps must be played with a good deal of fearlessness to overcome the natural tendency to tighten and thereby under-reach the interval distance. The middle section can be played quite *forte* and with driving energy. Although the only dynamic given is the *f* in m. 1, the overall dynamic plan should include good contrasts within a *mf* to *ff* range.

Prelude

The contrast between the steady, *legato* accompaniment in the left hand and the varied articulation in the right enhances the mysterious quality of this wonderful solo in G minor. The technical challenge for novice pianists is to maintain a strict *legato* in the left hand while observing the many different articulations in the melodic line. The twists and turns of the melody give it a quixotic, wry character; slight accents on the *staccato* downbeats (mm. 3, 6, 7, 8, etc.) will further enhance this ironic quality. It is wise to practice the brief canon in mm. 13–19 assiduously, so that no scale passage becomes muddled in performance. The alternating articulations between the hands here are challenging to work out, but once mastered, the climb to the *forte* high point at m. 17 is exciting and worth the effort!

Clowns

This very popular solo is often found in anthologies for the intermediate pianist, and its popularity is well deserved. The piece alternates between major and minor modes in an ironic, clumsy way, aptly conveying the character of the title. A student of mine once described this piece as "The one where the third finger can't decide what note to play." That characterization aptly conveys the humor of this great solo and is a perfect statement about why every student loves this piece: It is funny! One can easily imagine the slapstick antics of a circus clown in the irregular, angular phrases and awkward accents. The detailed articulation and repeated rhythmic figures in the melody contribute greatly to a successful performance of this delightful recital piece. All *staccato* and *legato* indications should be given their full due, and so too, the contrasting dynamic levels throughout.

Improvisation

This two-voice improvisation, reminiscent of J. S. Bach's two-part inventions, is the least known solo in Opus 39; it is also the most contemporary sounding solo in the set. Personally speaking, it was the most satisfying of the set to record because it called for a deeper intellectual and emotional commitment on my part. The writing is sparse, yet highly expressive, and sinuous. The performer needs a clear sense of line and musical maturity to convey the sophisticated character successfully. For that reason, I consider it the most challenging work in Opus 39, and it is not a work that will be readily understood by a young student. Full of unresolved tension and quirky phrases, this work has a mysterious personality that entices you as a performer and engages your musical curiosity. This is an excellent choice for a teen or adult student who is ready to take on a serious, mature piano work. It is also a good piece to assign to someone who may say he does not like contemporary music. Even as the most contemporary solo in this collection it is quite conservatively modern in style.

The right- and left-hand lines, like Bach's inventions, though dependent on each other harmonically, are independent melodically, and must be made meaningful, as independent melodies and as supportive harmonic structures. Here, as in many pieces where the melody is fragmented or not vocal in character, the performer must rely on his knowledge of harmony and instinctive musicianship to create a believable performance. I suggest practicing hands separate, so that each voice becomes a distinct personality, and each line has a destination. Tension points and periods of harmonic resolution must be identified and mapped out. For example, the seven-measure pedal point in mm. 12–18 plays a crucial role in the climax and gradual dissolution of harmonic tension, finally signaling the return to D minor at m. 19, the calm midpoint of the piece. In a piece such as this, the performer must envision the larger picture and always keep that in mind. Without this larger framework, the performance will lack focus and forward motion.

A Short Story

This beautiful solo moves along in a restless mood straight through to the end. In contrast to the previous piece, the high point of this solo is reached midway to the end. But here, too, a continuously rising melodic line and increasing dynamic levels signal the high point of the piece. The melody remains in the left hand throughout, punctuated by short, repeated motives in the right-hand accompaniment. This elegant study in double notes provides the novice pianist ample opportunity to master the art of playing double-note intervals and continuous blocked sixths as well. The contrasting articulations in each hand—a steady *legato* melody in the left hand accompanied by crisp, *staccato* double-notes in the right—make this an excellent study for the intermediate pianist. This rich solo also deserves a place on recital programs. Its graceful beauty is satisfying to play and hear.

Slow Waltz

This curious solo is quite humorous, and perhaps even a little sarcastic. The title, *Slow Waltz*, and the ungainly, lopsided melody provide fertile imagery for the performer. Like *Improvisation*, the sophisticated character of this solo requires mature pianism and a willingness to be a bit daring in performance. When I recorded this piece, the image that kept coming to mind was a festive, rural celebration where few dancing partners remain. The party is long over, but these lingering couples nonetheless continue to dance, long after everyone else has gone home, slowly turning around and around the dance floor in a funny, tired waltz. The performer should observe all the articulations carefully, especially when holding the right-hand notes while simultaneously playing the left-hand notes *staccato*, as in the first two measures. This detailed execution increases the impression of being not quite "in time" with the waltz rhythm. There is a certain elegance, as well, in holding the half note until the very last moment, delaying its release, and then reaching up quickly for the third-beat *staccato* note. The resulting "hiccup" lends a humorous, awkward quality to the melody.

A Happy Outing

On first glance, one might assume that the tempo marking *"Resoluto con brio"* indicates a brisk tempo. However, the busy quality of the melody and the bouncing left-hand accompaniment warrant a more moderate *"resoluto"* than a fast one. Above all, this solo must remain light and breezy, and a too fast tempo will not help this mood at all. The happy melody in E major chatters along, accompanied by a chordal left hand whose pattern is in reverse order—higher to lower—of the customary accompaniment pattern. This accompaniment contributes to the challenge of keeping this solo light-fingered.

A Happy Outing, Op. 39, No. 24, mm. 1-3, l.h.

Again, attention to all the details of articulation throughout the piece will make the solo come alive with character, and will make it sparkle. Kabalevsky has put many diverse ideas into this very short piece. The minor section beginning at m. 9 should contrast to the opening section and its return at the end. This section differs greatly from the first part, with its long *legato* melody and a left hand remarkably changed as well. It is important to play it quietly, as marked. This section is busy, like the rest of the solo, and the dynamic is more difficult to control. Underplaying the left hand slightly may help, and keeping the fingers very close to the keys may counteract a tendency to overplay these eighths in a faster tempo.

—*Margaret Otwell*

24 PIECES FOR CHILDREN

Opus 39

24 Pieces for Children

1. Melody

Dmitri Kabalevsky
Opus 39

2. Polka

3. Rambling

4. Cradle Song

5. Playing

Allegretto [poco scherzando]

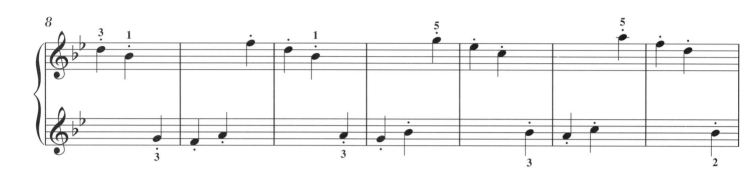

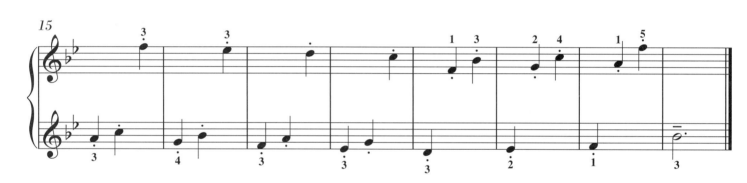

6. A Little Joke

7. Funny Event

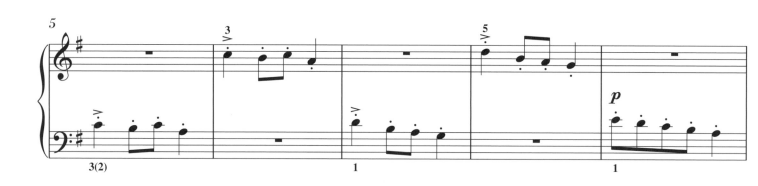

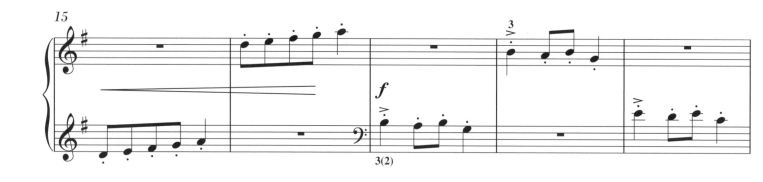

8. Song

9. A Little Dance

10. March

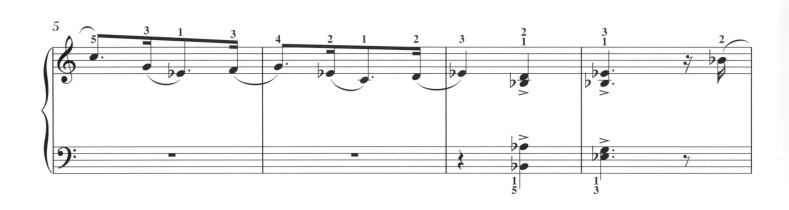

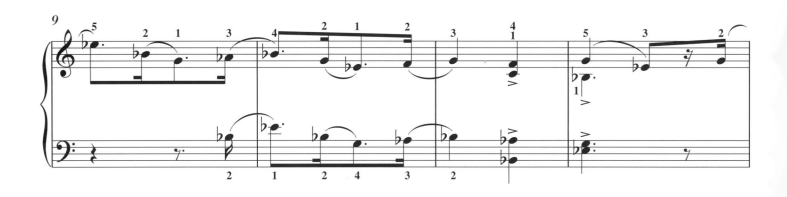

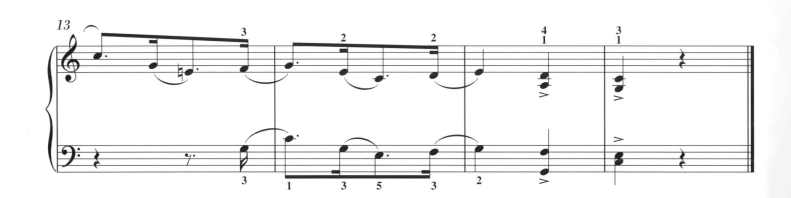

11. Song of Autumn

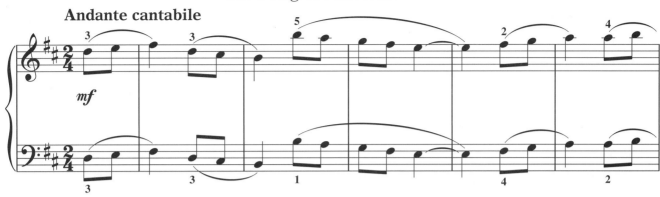

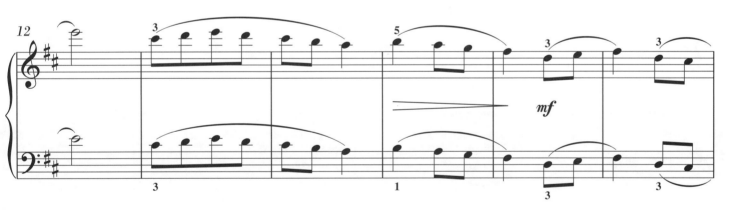

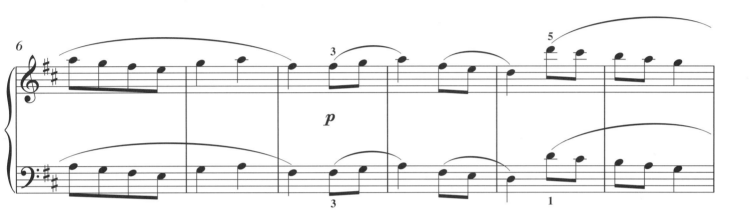

12. Scherzo

13. Waltz

14. A Fable

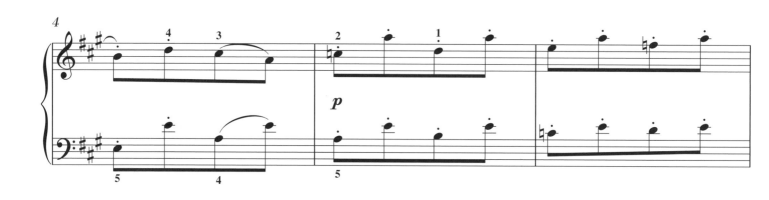

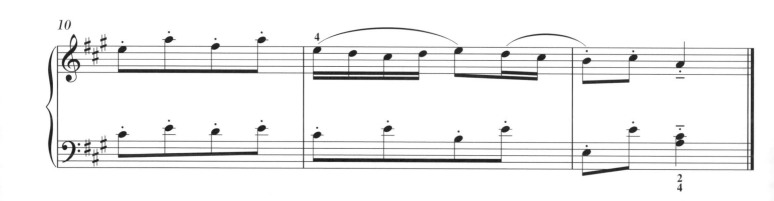

15. Jumping

16. A Sad Story

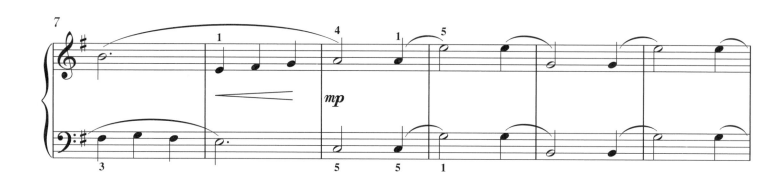

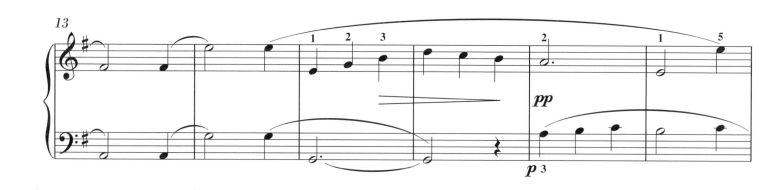

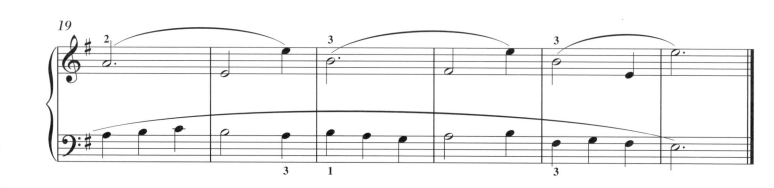

17. Folk Dance

18. Galop

19. Prelude

20. Clowns

21. Improvisation

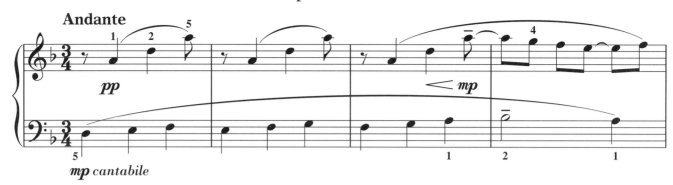

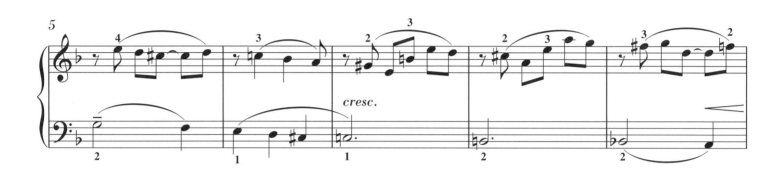

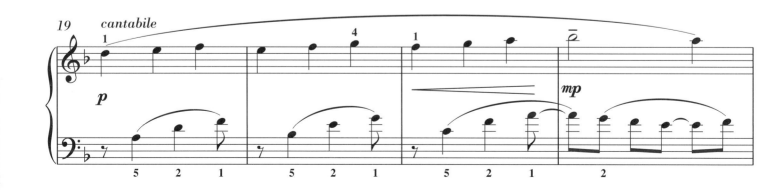

22. A Short Story

23. Slow Waltz

24. A Happy Outing

Resoluto con brio

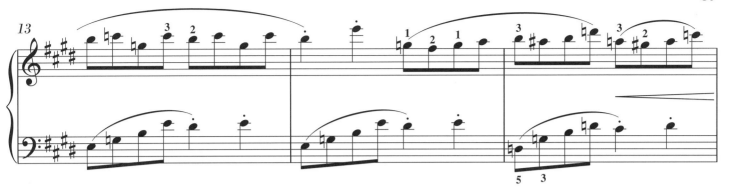

ABOUT THE EDITOR

MARGARET OTWELL

Margaret Otwell is a musician with a distinguished and varied career as a solo pianist, collaborative musician, and teacher. She has pursued an active role in educating young pianists as an independent piano teacher for over 25 years. A member of MTNA since 1978, she is a past president of the Northern Virginia Music Teachers Association, and has adjudicated for many piano competitions and events, including the Wolf Trap Young Artists Competition in Washington, DC and the National Piano Arts Competition in Milwaukee, WI. Dr. Otwell has served on the faculties of the University of Maryland Eastern Shore, The American University Preparatory Department, George Mason University, and the University of Wisconsin-Milwaukee.

As a pianist, Dr. Otwell is well known for her insightful interpretation of French piano repertoire. She has recorded the complete works of Déodat de Séverac for Musical Heritage Society Records. She has presented lecture-recitals, workshops, and master classes and has appeared in solo and chamber music performances throughout the United States, Canada, and Europe. Dr. Otwell was awarded a DMA degree in Performance from the University of Maryland, where she studied piano and pedagogy with Stewart Gordon, Thomas Schumacher, and Nelita True. She also studied piano with Gaby Casadesus as a recipient of a Fulbright performance grant to France.